This Book Belongs To

©2019 Rheo Gauthier

Enjoy coloring the pictures, but
please do not duplicate or distribute any
of the pages or images except
for personal, non-commercial use.

visit www.rheog.com

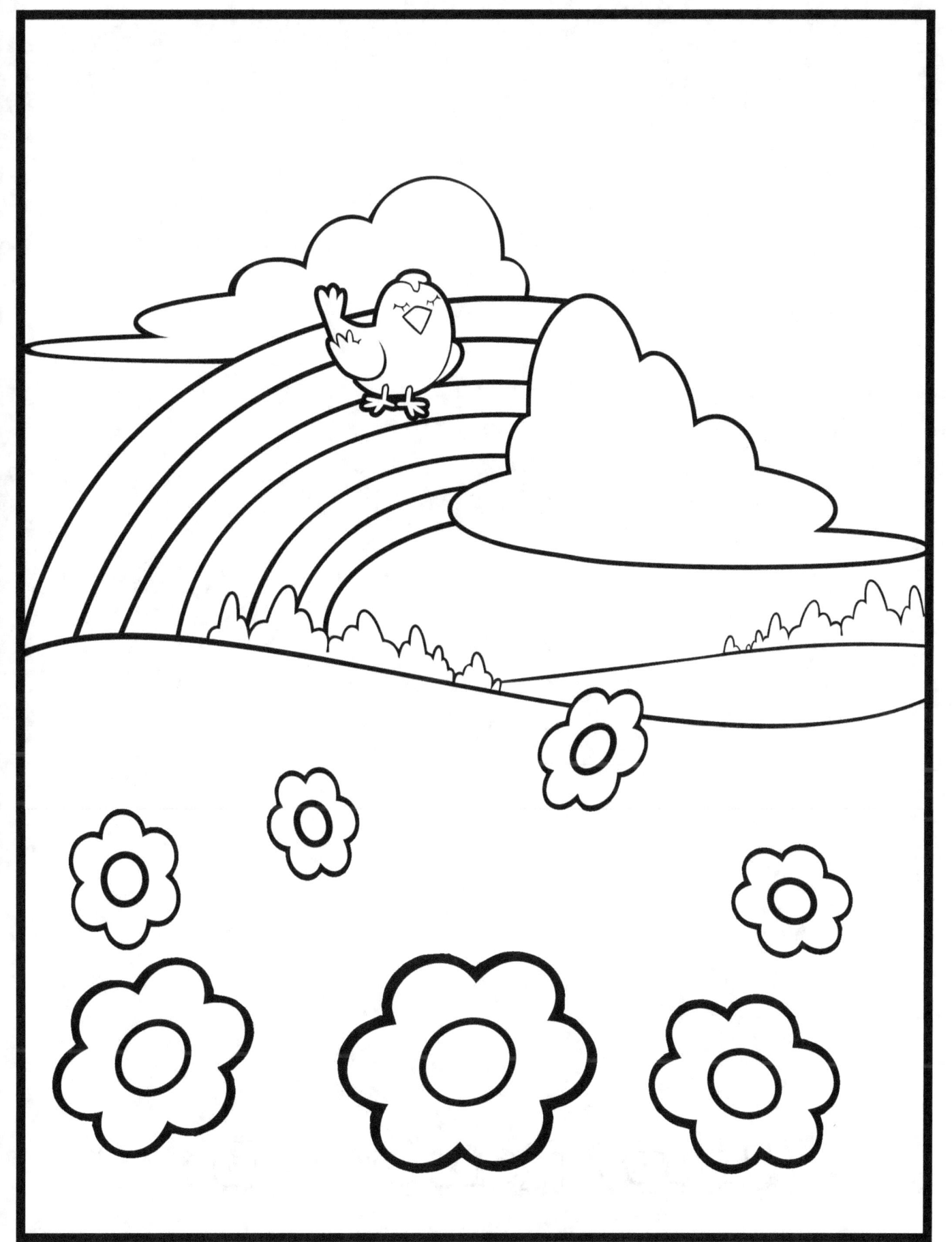

Happy Rainbow Bird

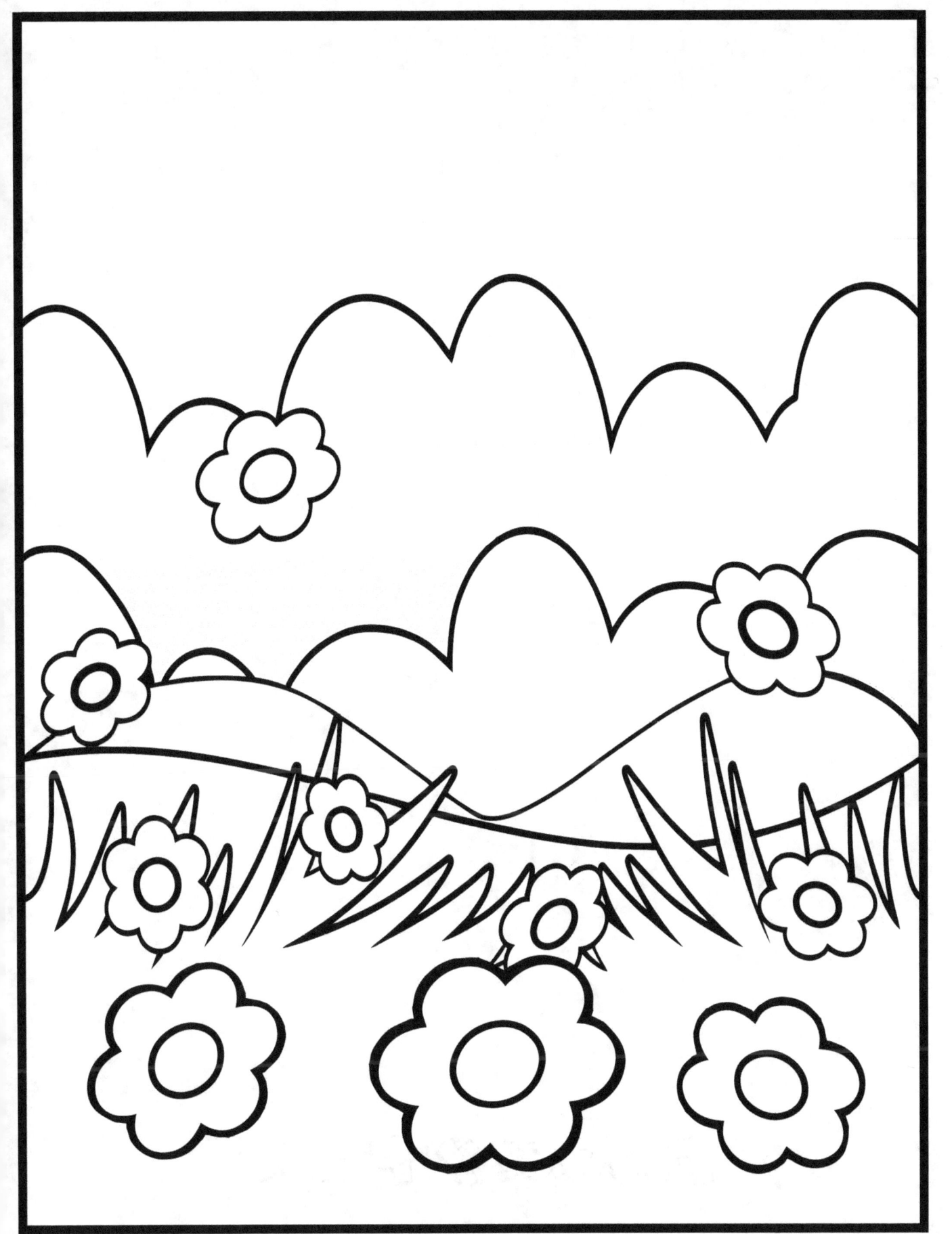

Flowery Field

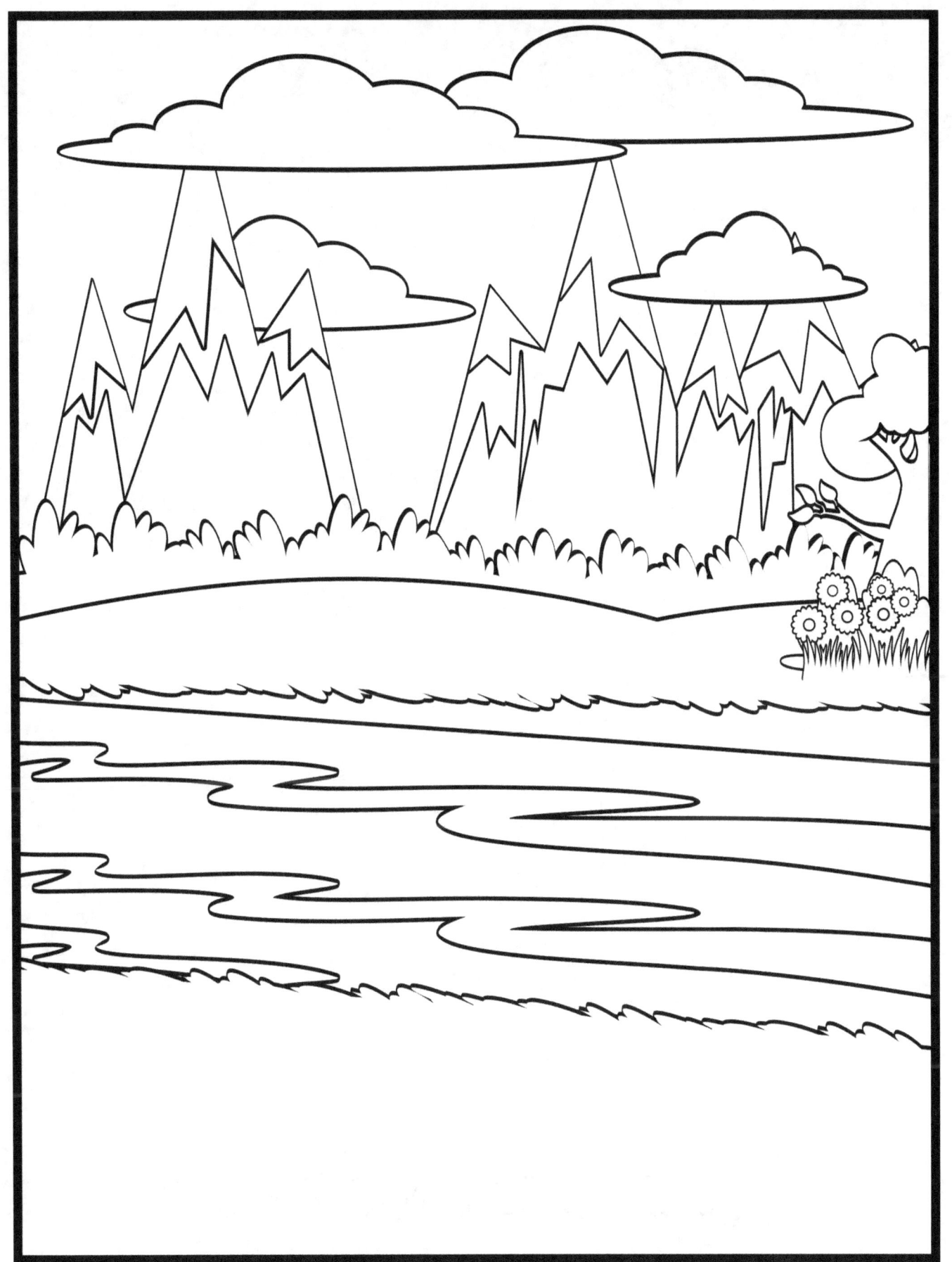

Mountain Stream

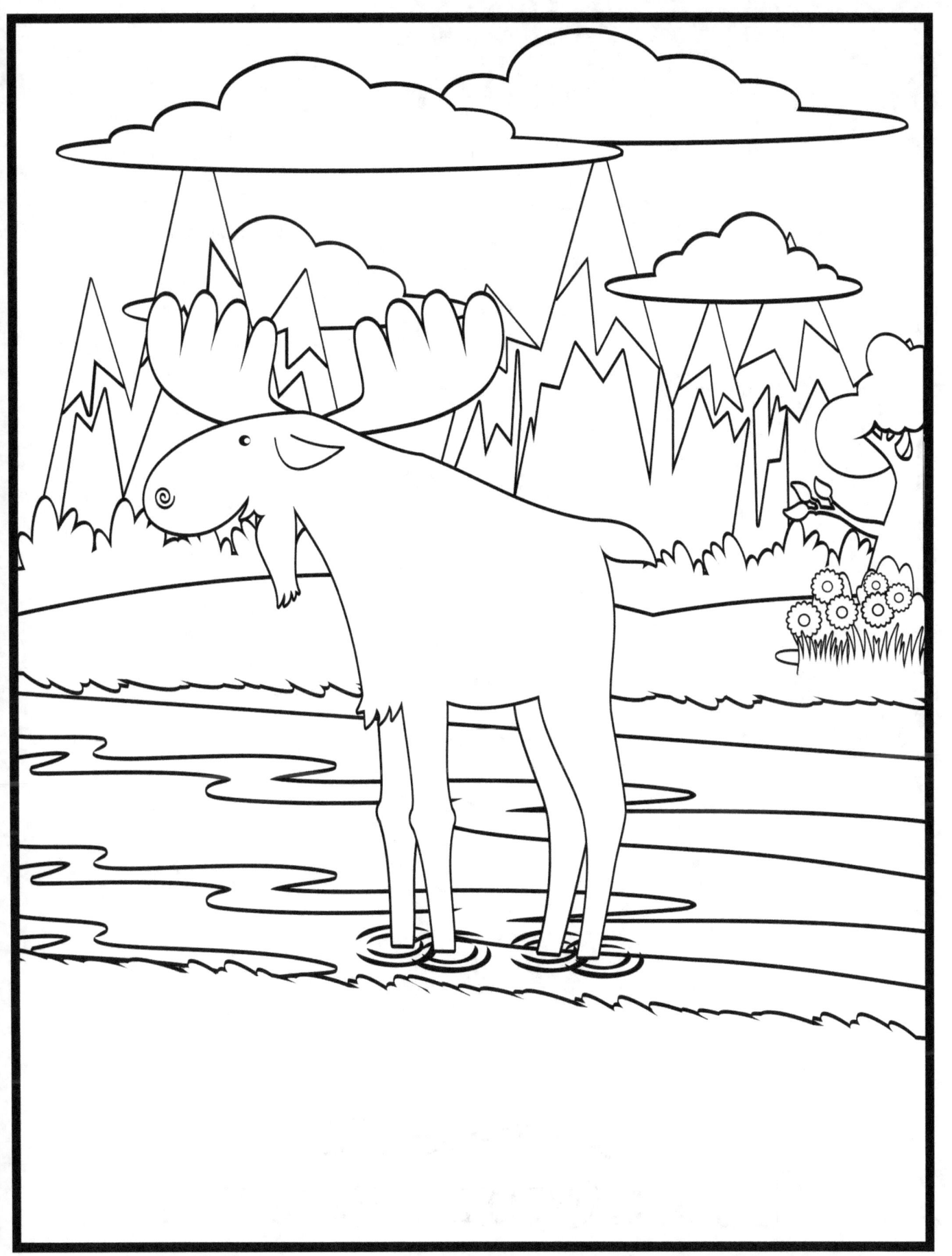

Moose in Mountain Stream

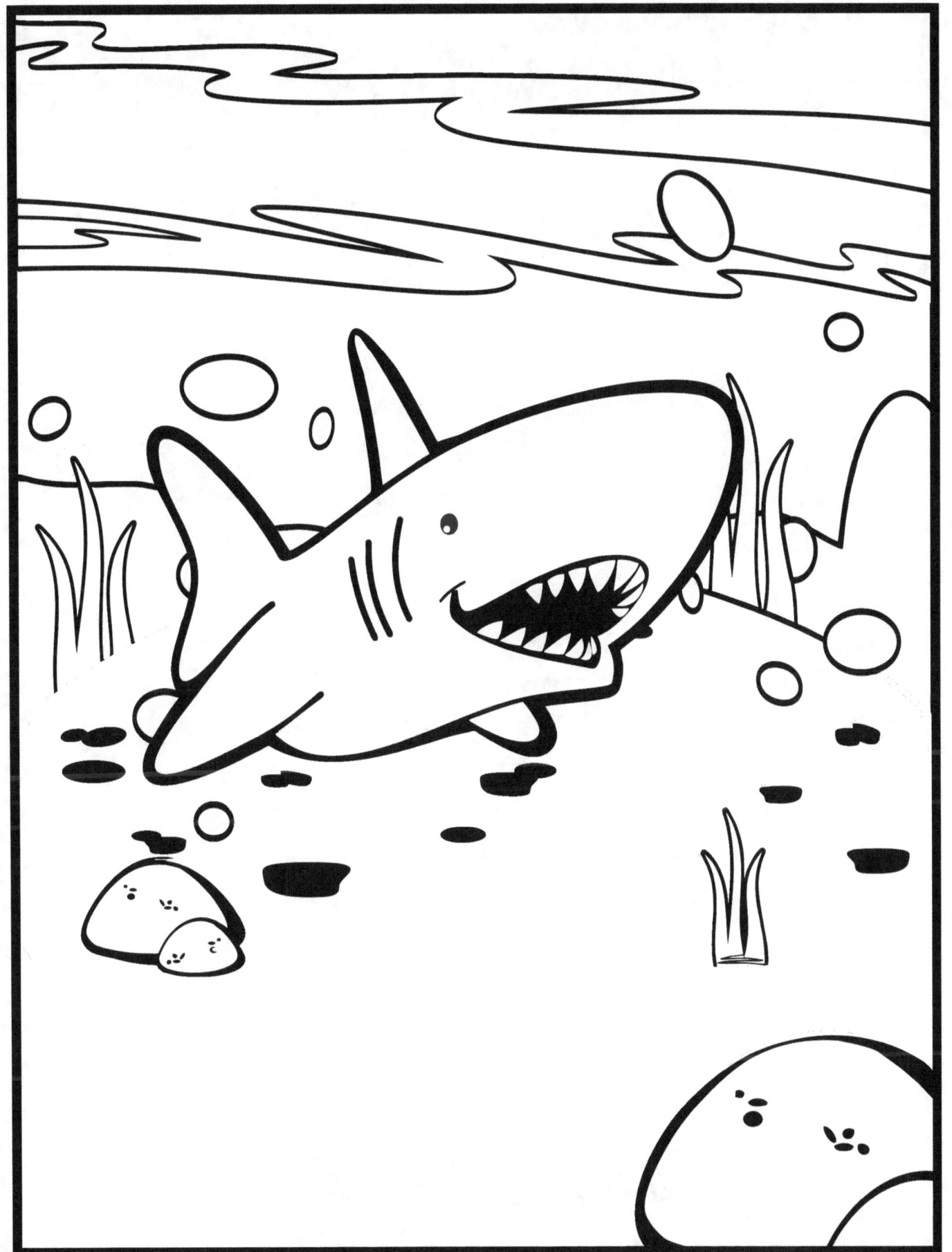

Happy Shark

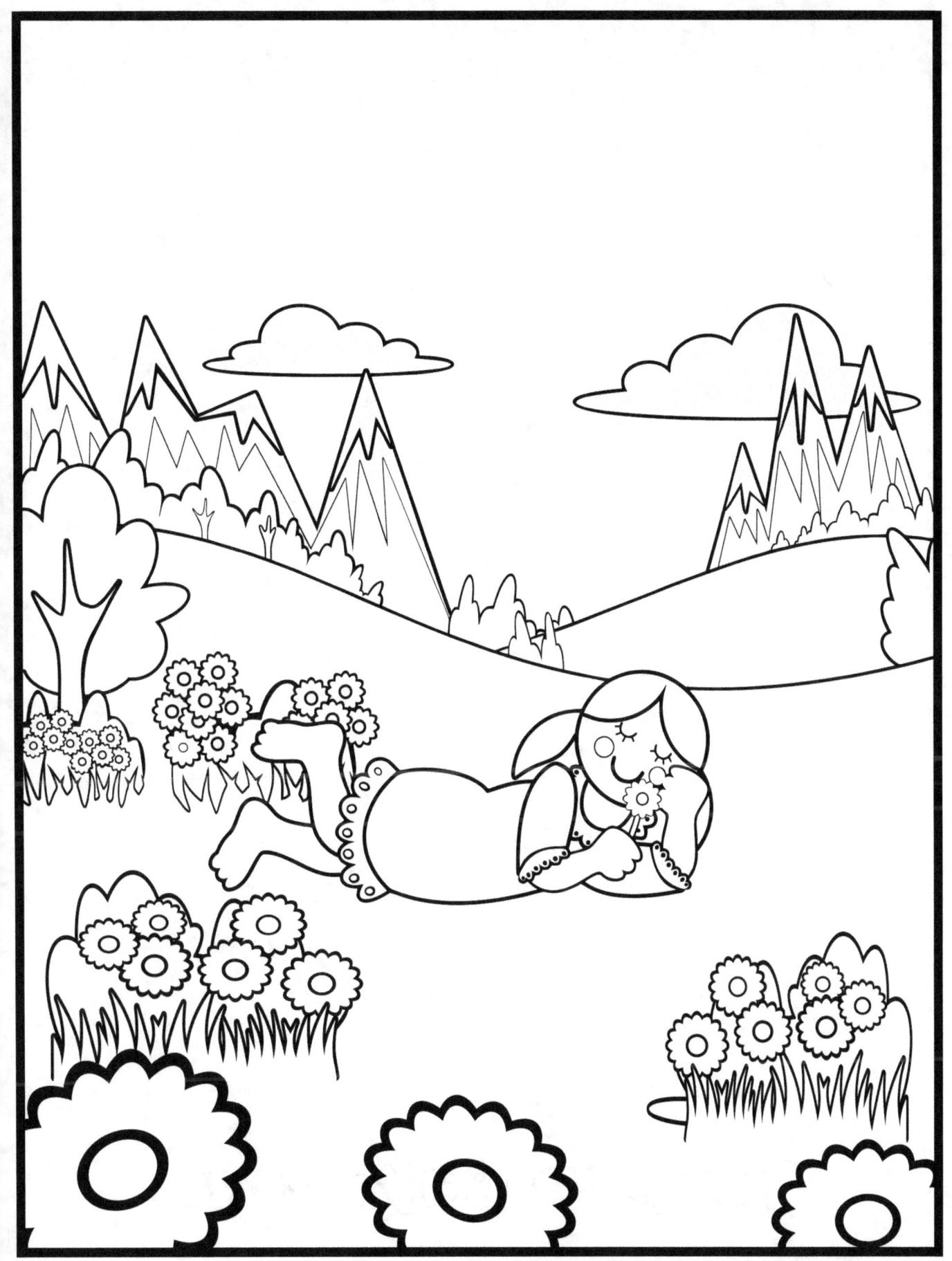

Summer Daydream

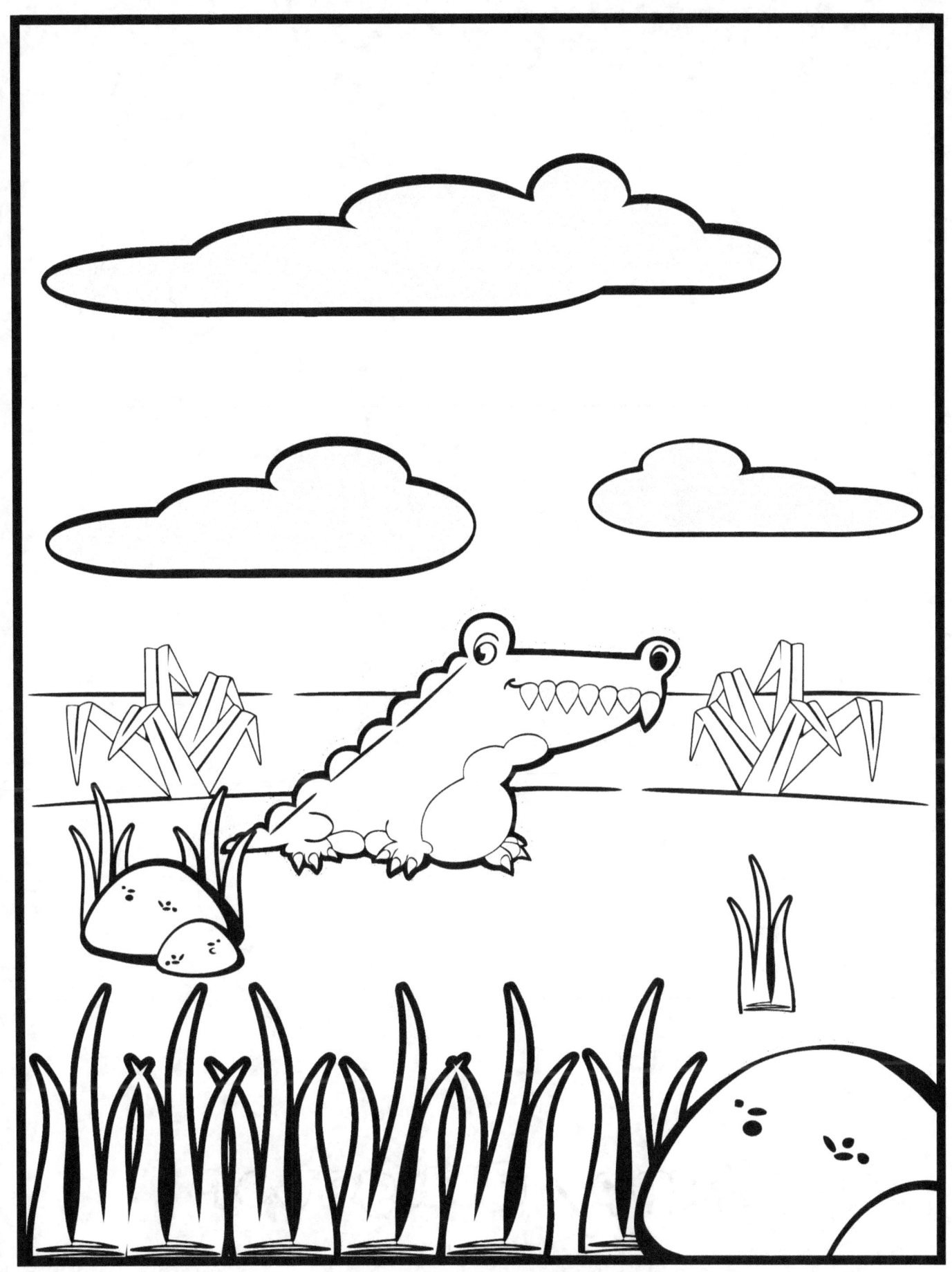

Happy Alligator

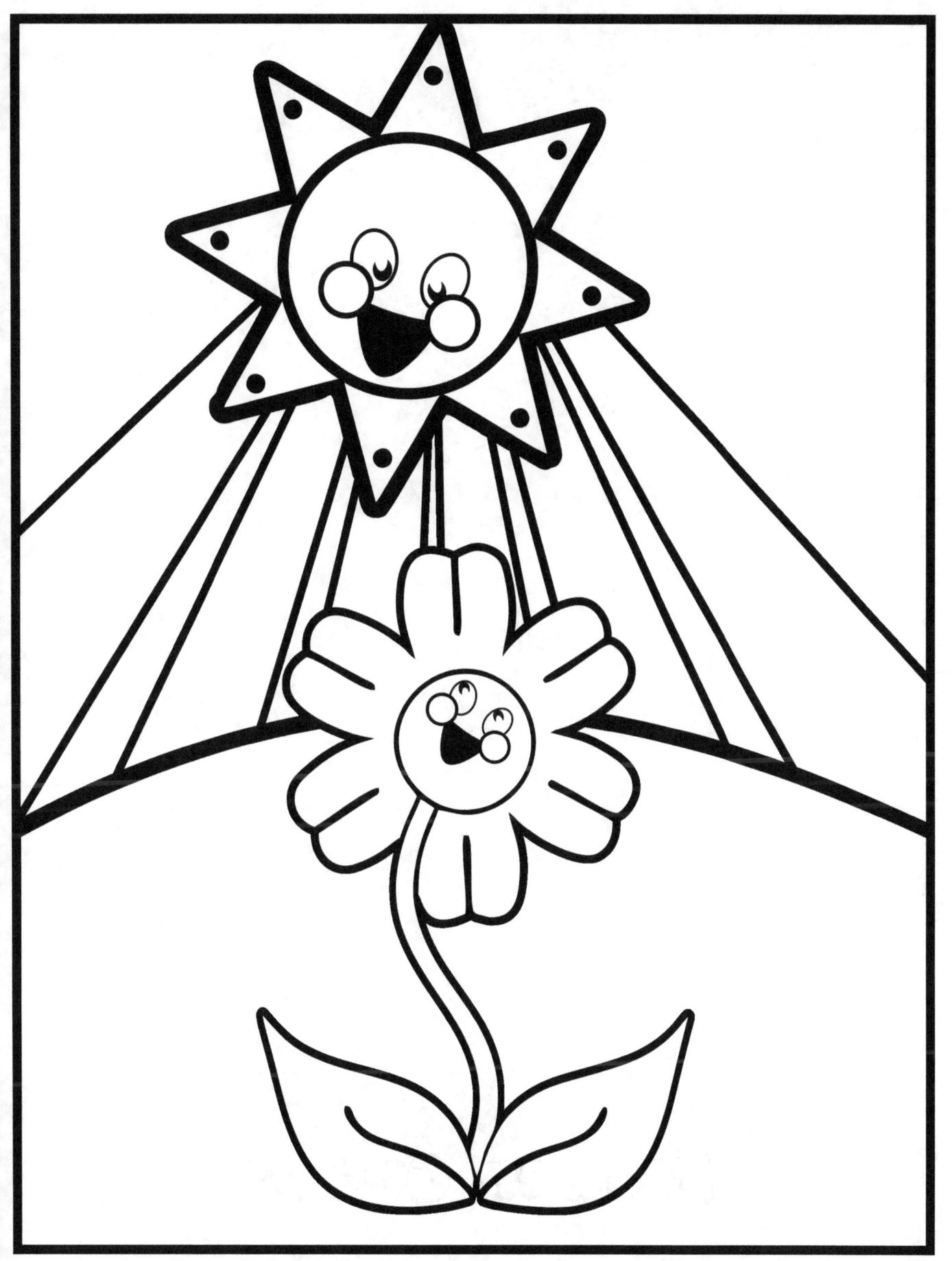

Flower Grows

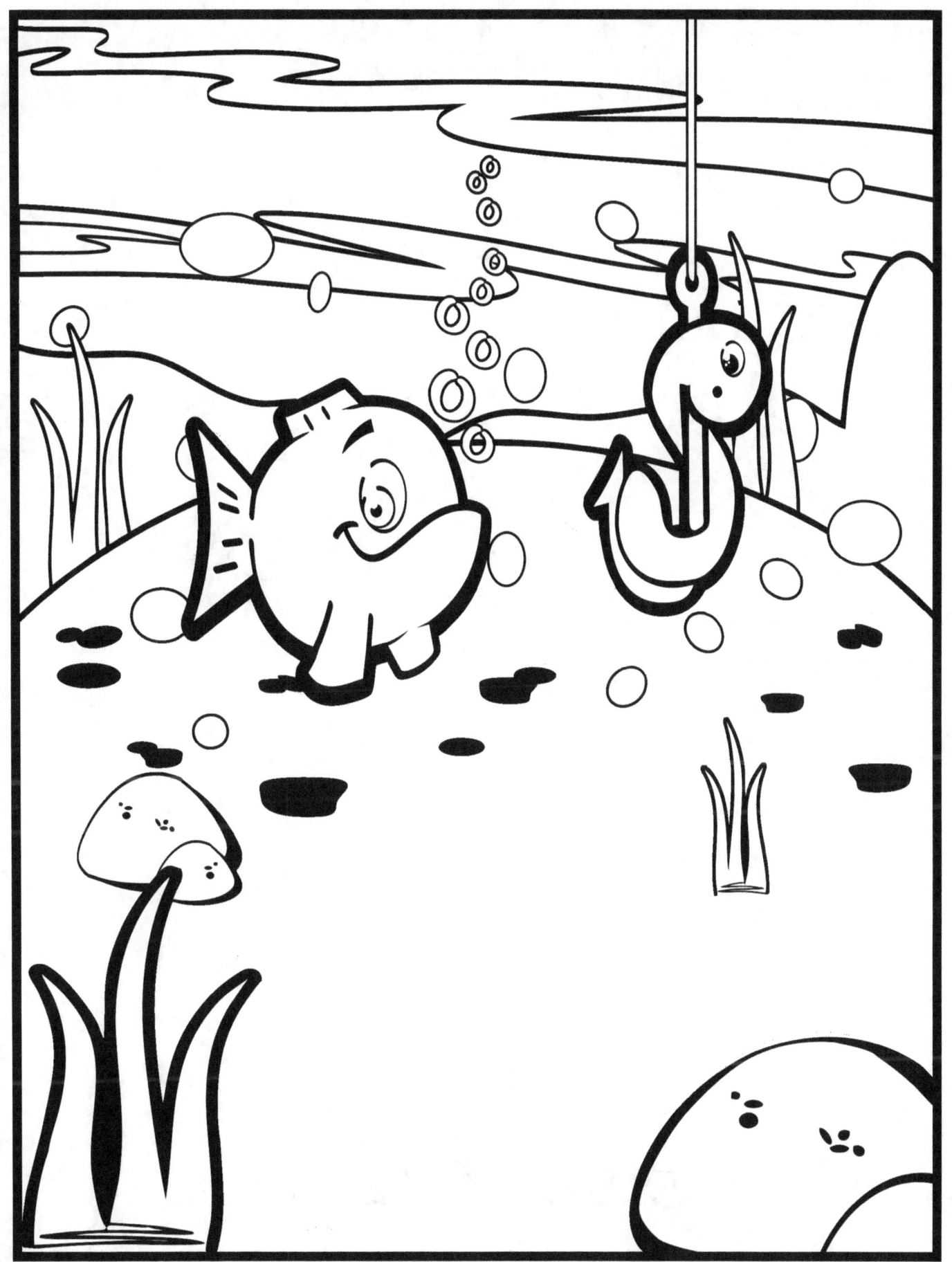

Gone Fishing

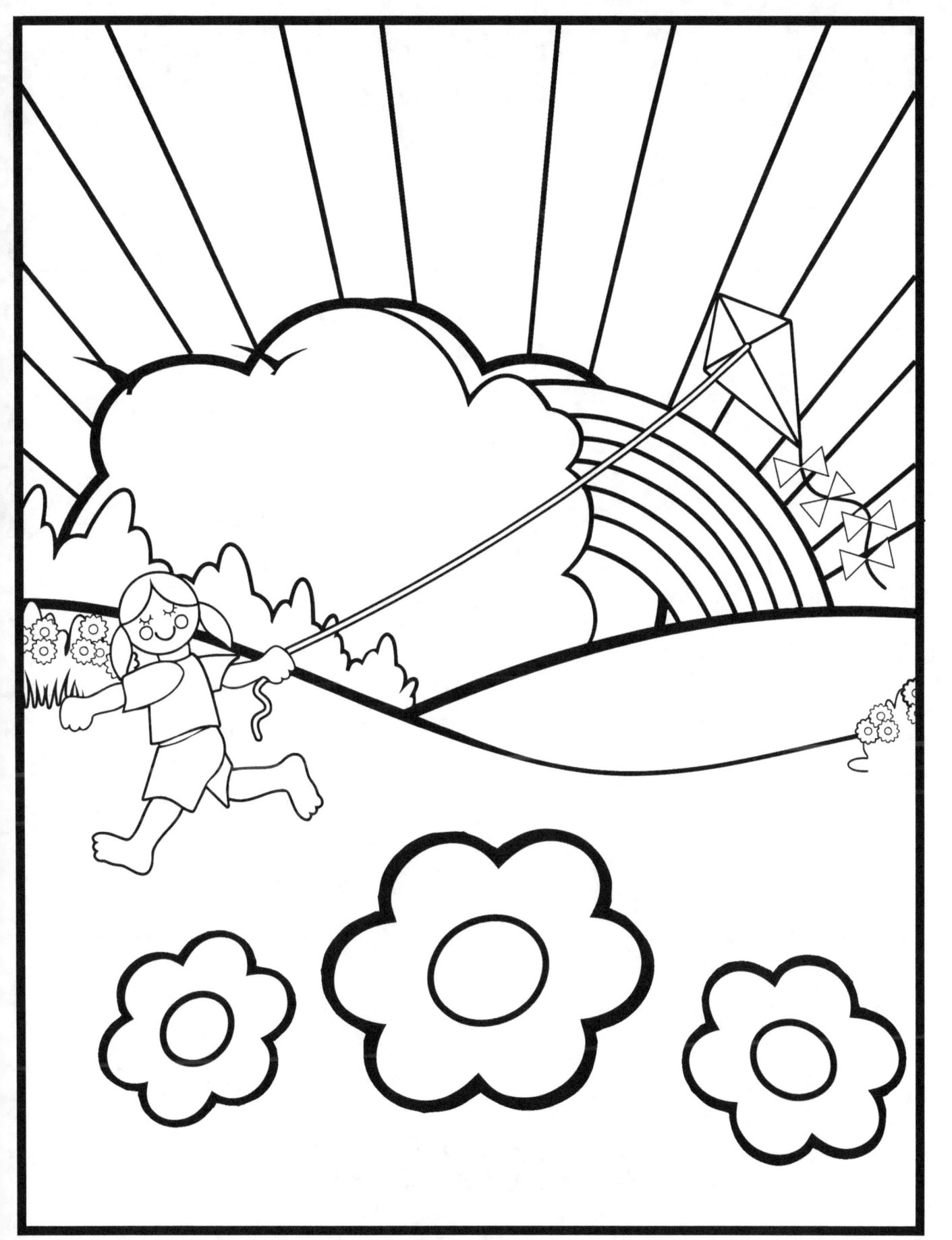

Happy Day

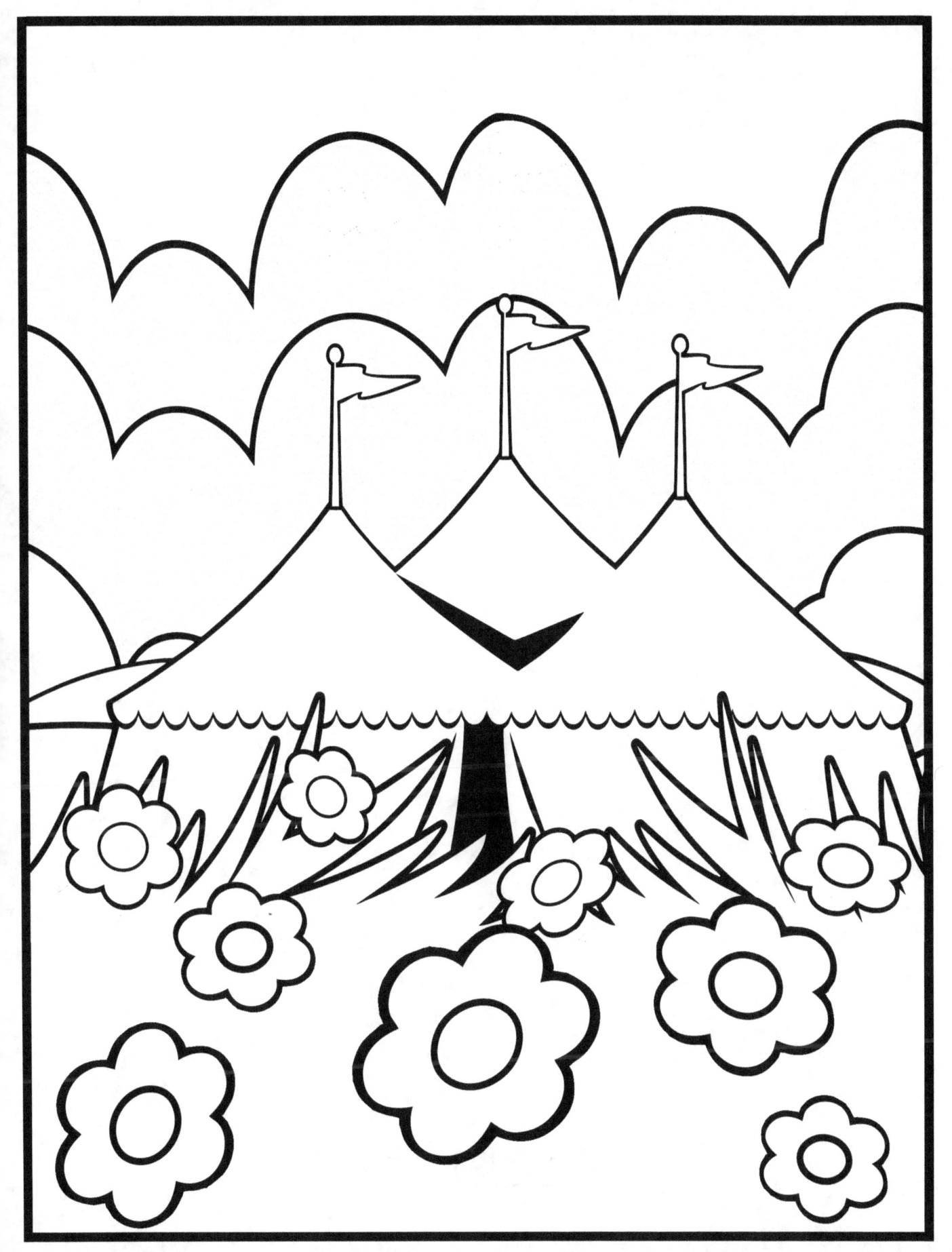

Circus Tent

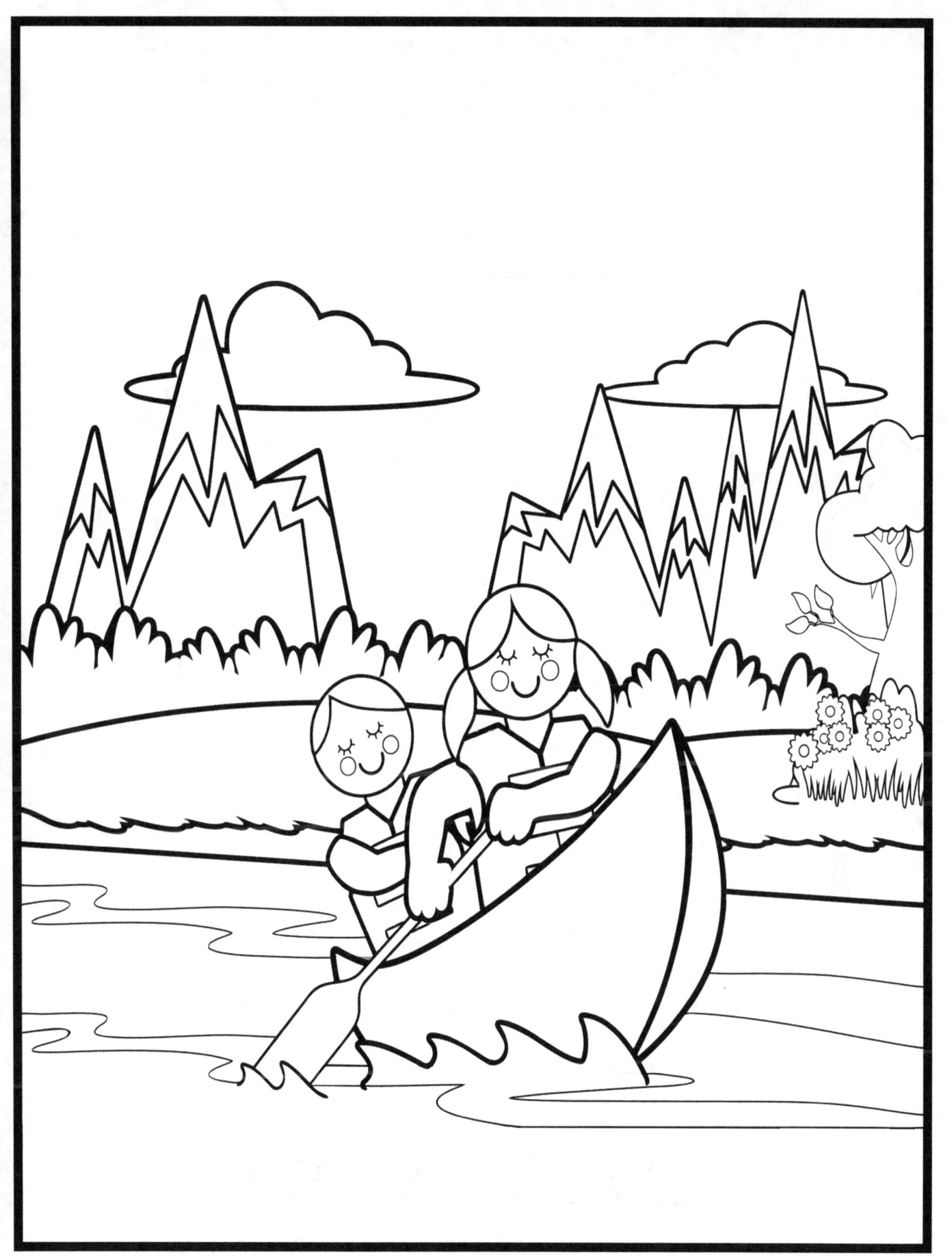

Up The Creek

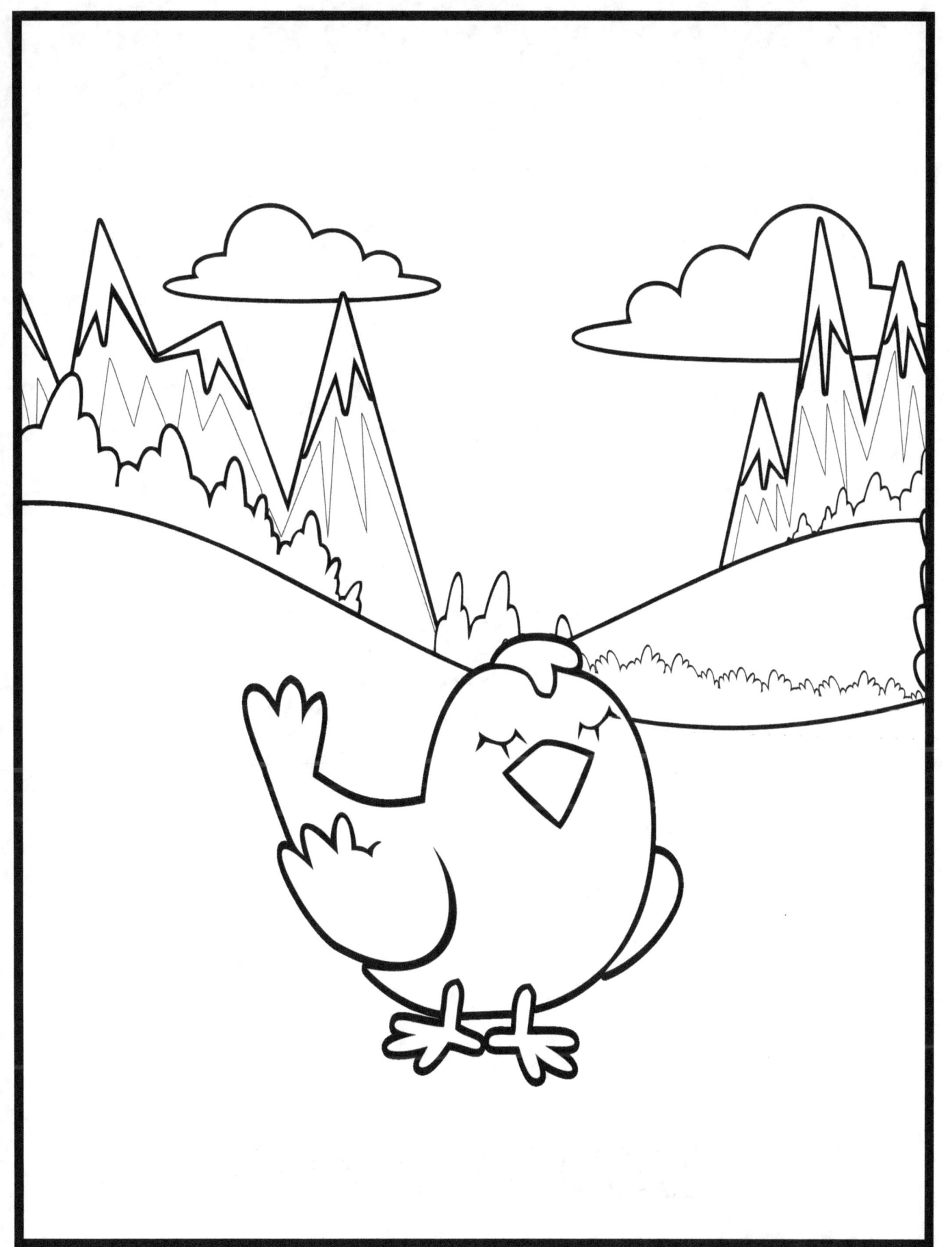

Life is Tweet

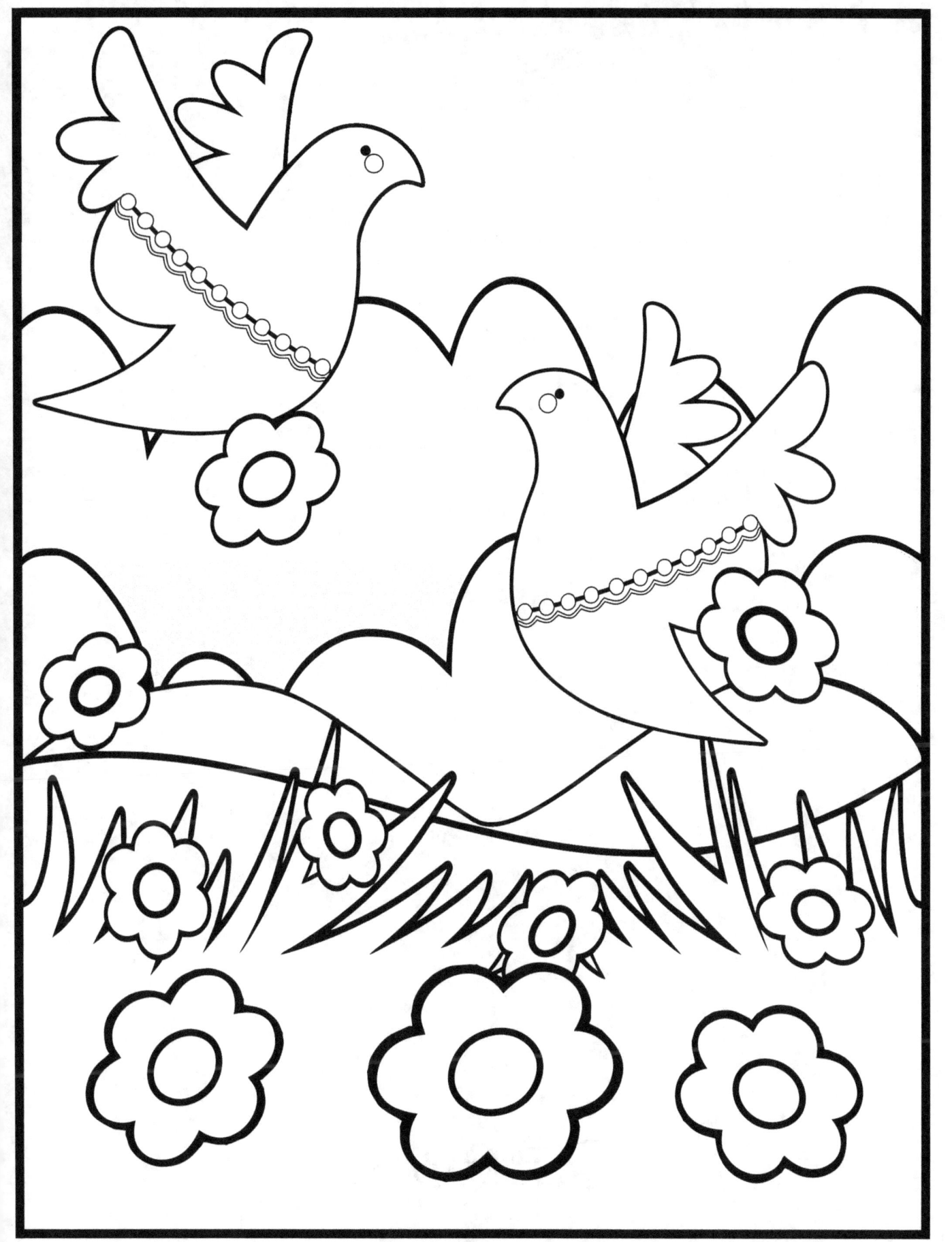

Flutter

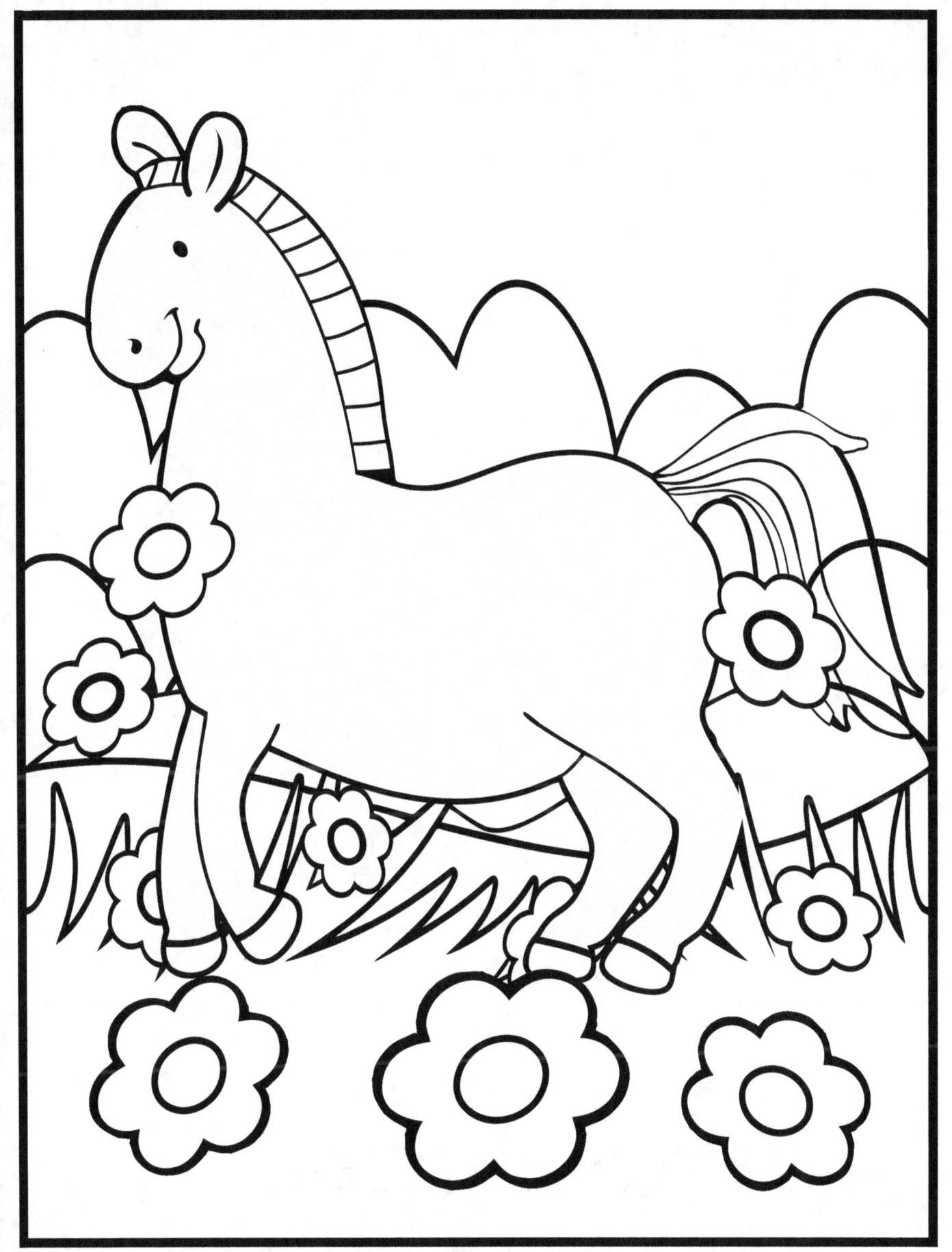

Wild Horse

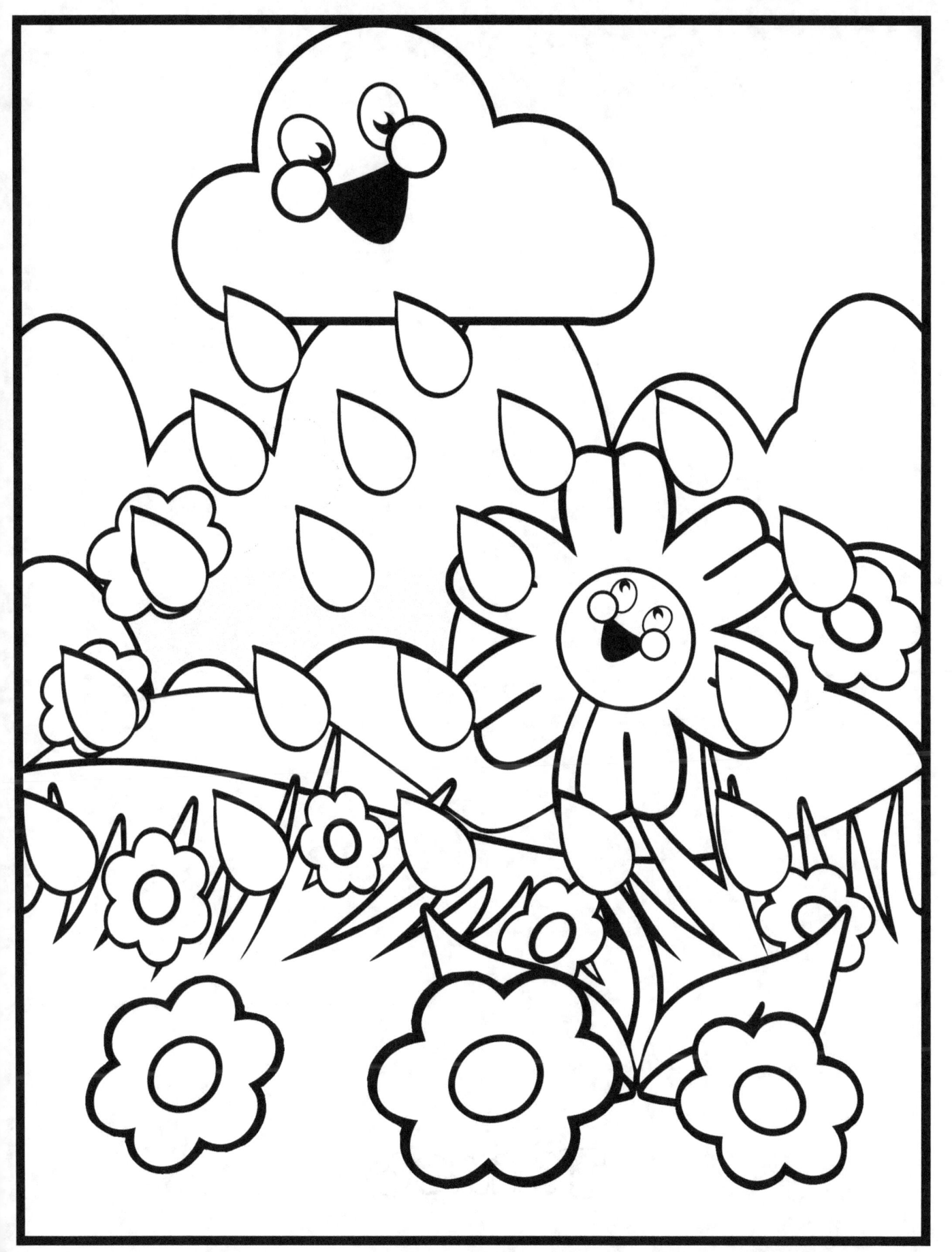

Thirsty

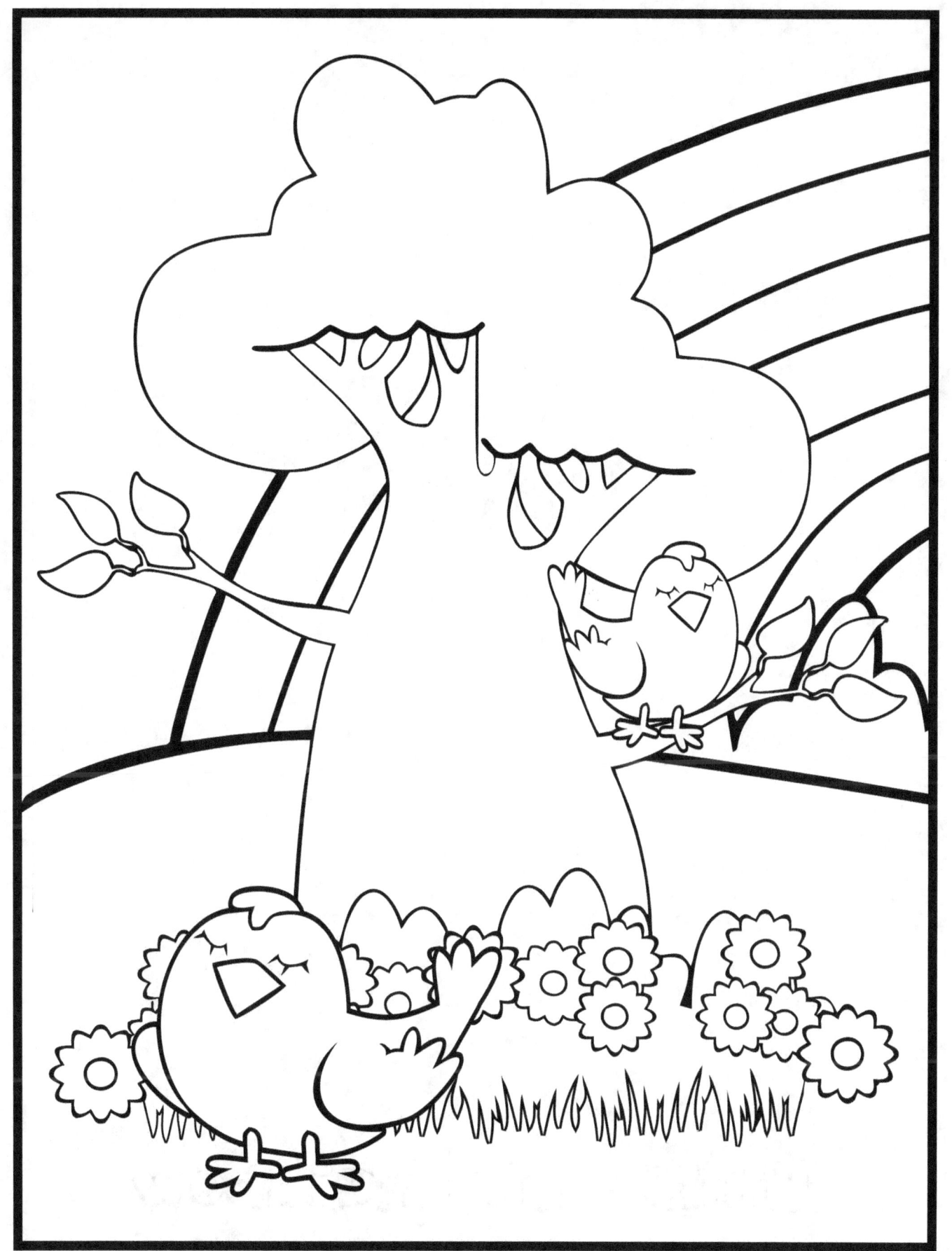

Under The Rainbow

www.ingramcontent.com/pod-product-compliance
Lightning Source LLC
Chambersburg PA
CBHW080816220526
45466CB00011BB/3586